The Jamestown C
□ With Writing Activities □

# Understanding Organization

Introductory Level

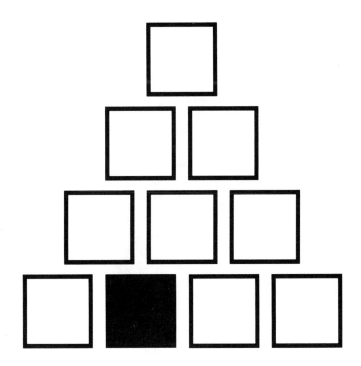

JAMESTOWN  PUBLISHERS

*a division of* NTC/CONTEMPORARY PUBLISHING COMPANY
Lincolnwood, Illinois USA

# Comprehension Skills Book

Understanding Organization
Introductory Level

ISBN: 0-89061-665-5

Published by Jamestown Publishers,
a division of NTC/Contemporary Publishing Company,
4255 West Touhy Avenue,
Lincolnwood (Chicago), Illinois 60646-1975 U.S.A.
© 1993 by NTC/Contemporary Publishing Company
This edition was prepared with the editorial assistance of Kraft & Kraft.
Cover and text design by Thomas Ewing Malloy.

7 8 9 0 C (S) 10 9 8 7 6 5 4 3 2

## Readability

Parts One and Two, Lesson:  Level C
Part Three, Sample Exercise:  Level C
Part Four, Practice Exercises:  Levels C–E
Passages 1–10:  Level C
Passages 11–20:  Level D
Passages 21–30:  Level E

# INTRODUCTION

The Comprehension Skills Series has been prepared to help students develop specific reading comprehension skills. Each book is completely self-contained. There is no separate answer key or instruction manual. Throughout the book, clear and concise directions guide the student through the lessons and exercises.

The titles of the Comprehension Skills books match the labels found on comprehension questions in other Jamestown textbooks. The student who is having difficulty with a particular kind of question can use the matching Comprehension Skills book for extra instruction and practice to correct the specific weakness.

Each book in the Comprehension Skills Series is divided into five parts.

1. Explanation: Part One clearly defines, explains, and illustrates the specific skill.

2. Instruction: Part Two offers an interesting and informative lesson presented in clear, readable language. A preview technique used regularly throughout Parts One and Two requires the student to anticipate and respond.

3. Sample Exercise: Part Three consists of a sample exercise with questions. For each question, the thinking of a student who answers correctly is modeled, the correct answer is explained, and the shortcomings of the other answers are pointed out. The sample exercise is designed to prepare the student for the work required in the following section. Students are urged to consult the instructor if they need extra help before proceeding to Part Four.

4. Practice Exercises: Part Four contains thirty practice exercises with questions. Edward Fry's formula for estimating readability was used to sequence the exercises. The passages begin at level C and advance gradually to level E. Students are advised to complete the thirty practice exercises thoughtfully and carefully.

5. Writing Activities: Part Five contains writing activities that help students apply the skills they have learned in earlier parts of the book. Many activities encourage students to work cooperatively with other students.

## HOW TO USE THIS BOOK

1. Read Part One, Organization and Understanding, which begins on page 5. Complete the Preview Quiz as you read.

2. Read Part Two, Methods of Organization, which begins on page 7. Complete the Preview Quizzes as you read.

3. Complete the Sample Exercise in Part Three, which begins on page 15. Read and follow the instructions carefully. After you have completed the exercise, read the explanation following it.

4. Complete the thirty Practice Exercises in Part Four, which begins on page 19. Read and follow the instructions carefully.

5. Complete the Writing Activities, which begin on page 51. Read and follow the instructions carefully. After you complete each activity, your teacher may want to discuss your answers with the class.

6. Use the Answer Key, which begins on page 59, to correct your answers after you complete each exercise.

7. Record your progress on the chart on the inside back cover.

# *Organization and Understanding*

### Speed or Meaning?

Some people stress reading for speed. But good reading means understanding, not speed. Quick reading may not be good reading. A slow reader may understand more.

We all would like to read fast *and* well. For most of us this won't work. Some things are easy to read. Others are hard. For that reason, we have to shift speeds. A science book is full of facts. It must be read slowly. A comic novel has a lively pace. It can be read quickly.

Some writing is easy to understand. Some is hard. Why? Some requires more thinking. The harder the writing, the harder your mind must work.

A reader has two basic jobs. One is to recall details. The other is to grasp ideas. Some people skip facts, figures, and details. They don't want to slow down to make mental notes. Others stop at facts. They try to memorize them. Neither way is good reading. Good readers shift speed. They slow down for key facts and details. They speed up for minor details. Their technique is good.

# How Organization Helps You

Good reading means more than recalling facts. Reading takes many skills. One skill is seeing how the facts are arranged. This book will show you how facts are organized. You will learn how to find key facts. You will see what they add to meaning. You will learn how to summarize them.

A summary is a short version of a passage. Summaries make details easy to recall. They can also help you see how facts are related.

A summary should follow the author's pattern. First, you must see that pattern. Read this passage.

> Last night's fire took the lives of two children. They were trapped in the building. Five fire fighters were hurt in the blaze. Damage reached a million dollars. Two buildings burned down. The YMCA building was also damaged.

The facts are in order of importance. Deaths are first. Then come injuries. Damage to property is last. Why are property losses last? People are more important than buildings. Here is a good summary.

> Last night's fire killed two children, hurt five fire fighters, and did a million dollars' worth of damage.

# PART TWO

# *Methods of Organization*

### Preview Quiz 2

As a preview of Part Two, try to answer this question:

Details support ideas. How are details organized?
- ☐ a.  in no order
- ☐ b.  in a pattern that suits the topic
- ☐ c.  in any way

Begin reading Part Two to find the answer.

### Introduction

This part will expand the ideas in Part One. We will discuss these things:

- how writers organize facts
- how organization can help you
- how to make summaries

### Forms for Details

Writers don't let their thoughts wander aimlessly. They think logically. They organize details in patterns. A pattern is a form for ideas. The best form suits the topic. It helps the writer achieve his or her purpose for writing.

Six forms are widely used. They are listed at the top of the next page.

1. simple listing
2. order of importance
3. time order
4. space order
5. cause and effect
6. comparison and contrast

## Simple Listing

Listing details is easy for the writer. But it isn't always easy for a reader to understand.

Simple listing is the loosest form. Authors use it when no other form seems to fit. They just put one detail after another. There is no real attempt to arrange them. All the details seem to be equal. None stands out as more important. That is one thing that the form says. "All the details are equal. Not one detail is more important than another."

## Order of Importance

Order of importance means that some details are more important than others. Major ideas are stressed more than minor ones. Usually, the most important detail comes first. Minor ones follow it.

Sometimes writers reverse the pattern. They build to the most important detail, which comes last. You may see this pattern in an argument. The writer has many points to make. One is the strongest. The writer wants the key point to stay in the reader's mind. That's why it comes last.

Often writers signal the importance of the details. They do this with words and phrases. These include *most importantly* and *of greatest importance.*

How should you summarize writing organized by order of importance? Focus on the major ideas. Skip the minor ones.

## Time Order

Time order is used for stories. The story may be fact or fiction. Time order tells "what happened when."

Events are usually stated as they occurred. But a writer may change this order. The story may flashback, or recall events from the past. We see events that shaped the present. The story may "flash-forward" to the future. We see the results of present events. We see their importance.

Notice the order of events. That will help you recall them. To sum up a time-order passage, list the key events. Keep them in order.

Sometimes dates are important. This is often true in history books. Don't try to recall each date by itself. You will find that too hard. Make the dates part of a summary. Then you will see where they fit. You will find them easier to recall.

## Space Order

Space order is the basic form for description. It is based on where things are. Here's how it works.

The writer looks at a scene. (In fiction, the writer imagines the scene.) Next, the writer lists details. The list helps you "see" the scene. For instance, the writer may start with the farthest object. One by one, he or she moves to the nearest. Or the writer may move from right to left. Any order will work *if it makes sense.* The writer should try to shape the description so that you can follow it.

Space order may be used to describe a person. The author might start with a striking detail, such as piercing eyes. From the eyes, he or she moves to lesser details. Or the writer might start with lesser details. He or she builds up to the striking detail.

> Martin was a thin boy. His skin was pale. Broad shoulders saved him from looking weak. His hair and eyes were black. When he lifted his head, his right eyebrow rose and trembled.

When you summarize a passage written in space order, try to get an overall view. Include the key details. If there is one striking detail, be sure to put that in. Leave out minor details.

> Martin was thin and pale with black hair and eyes. His right eyebrow trembled.

## Preview Quiz 4

Try to answer this question:

Which sentence shows cause-and-effect organization?
☐ a. People are homeless because of the fire.
☐ b. These towels are on sale.
☐ c. Rain fell all day.

Continue reading to find the answer.

## Cause and Effect

You know that one thing may make another happen. A **cause** makes an event happen. An **effect** is the event itself. It is the result. The cause brings about the effect.

Here is an example of cause and effect:

> Because of the fire, people are homeless.

This sentence shows one cause and one effect. The pattern is easy to see. It is stated directly.

The pattern may be reversed.

> People are homeless because of the fire.

The effect is first. The cause follows. Often this pattern is harder to see. The parts may be separated. The cause may be stated at the start. The effect may not come until the end.

> Fire swept through Kingston. High winds fanned the flames. Many buildings burned. Alarms rang in nearby towns. People were left homeless.

To sum up cause and effect paragraph organization, you must include the cause and the effect. You may leave out other details.

## Comparison

A comparison shows how things are alike. Comparison helps explain something unfamiliar. For example, a writer can explain a robot by comparing it to a person.

To sum up a comparison, show how the two are alike.

## Contrast

A contrast shows how things differ. A writer might show how a hawk differs from an eagle. That is contrast.

To sum up a contrast, show the main differences.

## Comparison and Contrast

Comparison and contrast can work together. They may be used in the same passage. Suppose a writer is discussing gold and silver. First, he or she might show their likenesses. Next, he or she might show their differences.

Why do writers use comparison and contrast? They may just want to show a likeness or difference. More often they use comparison and contrast to make a larger point.

The things being compared or contrasted are often linked. Key words link them. They may help you spot this pattern. Here are some key words.

| | |
|---|---|
| either . . . or | some . . . others |
| not only . . . but also | both . . . and |

These pairs show likeness or difference.

## Combinations

An author may use one pattern for a topic. Or an author may use more than one pattern. One passage may use two or three patterns.

Read the next passage. It combines forms. See if you can find the patterns as you read.

> The first Madison Square Garden was in the heart of old New York. It had a spacious stage. Its big open arena was framed by a U-shaped gallery. In the fall of 1886, a clang of hammers filled the old arena. On the huge floor, carpenters built a frontier landscape. Perched on lofty ladders, painters sketched a mountain scene. They were getting the Garden ready for Buffalo Bill's Wild West Show. Today's Madison Square Garden is much larger. It is far from Madison Square. Yet it keeps the name of New York's first huge indoor arena.

The passage uses two patterns. The old Garden is described in space order. So are the preparations for the Wild West Show. The old and new Gardens are contrasted. Each pattern suits some facts. We can sum up the passage this way:

> The first Madison Square Garden was U-shaped with a huge stage. Buffalo Bill's Wild West Show was held there, using frontier scenery. Today's Madison Square Garden is larger and in a different place.

## Summary

Understanding organization will improve your reading skill. Making summaries will help you recall what you read. These five steps can help you.

1. Find the main idea.
2. Find the main details.
3. See how details are related.
4. See which pattern of organization is used.
5. Summarize the passage.

This lesson showed you how to follow a writer's organization. It showed you how to make summaries. Remembering facts and details is not enough. You must see how they are related.

The sample exercise that follows will let you practice what you learned in this lesson. Read it carefully. Refer back to these pages if you need to.

# PART THREE

# *Sample Exercise*

On the next page is a sample exercise. It shows how to use what you have learned in Parts One and Two.

The sample also previews the thirty exercises in Part Four. Read the sample passage and answer the sample questions. That will get you off to a good start.

The answers to the questions are explained. You will find out why the correct answers are the best answers. You will see where the wrong answers are faulty. The text also tells how you might think as you work through the exercise correctly.

Finish the sample carefully. Give it some thought. Do not go on to Part Four until you are sure you understand organization and how to summarize what you read.

## Sample Exercise

A hush fell over the plant. Machines ground to a halt. Conveyor belts whirred slower and then stopped. Soon the only sounds were made by the workers. They moved to the end of the assembly line. They whispered excitedly to each other. This was a great moment. The whispers quieted. The workers gathered around the car at the end of the line. One of them cranked the car into life. Another drove the car carefully out the factory door.

The workers broke into wild cheering. They tossed their caps into the air. The factory whistle screamed. The reason? Ransom Olds, the inventor of the Oldsmobile, had just produced his two-thousandth car. He had overtaken the industry leader, Colonel Pope, and his best-selling electric model.

1. In the first paragraph, the author arranges details by
   ☐ a. order of importance.
   ☐ b. space order.
   ☐ c. cause and effect.
   ☐ d. time order.

2. The workers cheered and tossed their caps because
   ☐ a. the factory had closed.
   ☐ b. Colonel Pope had just bought the company.
   ☐ c. the conveyor belts had stopped.
   ☐ d. Olds had just produced his two-thousandth car.

3. In the last paragraph, the author arranges details by
   ☐ a. simple listing.
   ☐ b. comparison.
   ☐ c. cause and effect.
   ☐ d. space order.

4. Underline a sentence that tells what had to be done before a man could drive the car out the factory door.

## *Answers and Explanations*

1. First, notice the details. Then notice how they are arranged. In this case, each sentence tells one event. One event happens after another. You should see that the best answer is *d.* This paragraph is organized by time order. It tells "what happened when."

   Answer *a* is wrong. One event *is* most important. It is the last. A man drove the car out the door. But the other events are also important. One is as important as the next. They are arranged by time, not importance.

   Answer *b* is wrong. This paragraph does not describe where things are in the factory. For example, we don't know where the door is.

   Answer *c* is wrong. The writer doesn't show why these things are happening. The next paragraph tells us that.

2. First, decide which of the choices is suggested in the paragraph. Read the choices, and then review the paragraph to see which of them makes sense. The best answer is *d.* The writer shows us some events. Then the writer gives the cause of those events. The writer even uses key words to show the cause.

   The reason? Ransom Olds, the inventor of the Oldsmobile, had just produced his two-thousandth car.

   Answer *a* is wrong. It does not refer to an event in the passage. The factory didn't close.

   Answer *b* is wrong. It does not even state something that is likely. Olds is competing with Colonel Pope.

   Answer *c* is wrong. There would be no reason for the workers to cheer if the conveyor belts had stopped. This is not a cause. It is another effect. The conveyor belts stopped as part of the celebration.

3. Again, you must decide the organization. First, notice the details. Then notice how they are arranged. The first three sentences tell what happened. The next two sentences tell why. You should see that the best answer is *c.* The writer uses cause and effect. The workers cheered because the two-thousandth car was built. That's why they tossed their caps. That's why the whistle screamed.

Answer *a* is wrong. The writer does not simply list details at random. We see the effects first. Then we see the cause.

Answer *b* is wrong. The writer does not compare things. For example, he or she does not compare the Oldsmobile and Colonel Pope's car.

Answer *d* is wrong. This paragraph does not describe where things are happening.

4. To find the sentence, skim the passage. First, find the sentence about driving the car out the factory door.

Another drove the car carefully out the factory door.

Now look at the sentences that tell about what happened *before* that. Find the one that tells what *had* to be done.

One of them cranked the car into life.

That is the correct answer. Old-fashioned cars were started with a crank.

Did you have trouble answering these questions correctly? If so, read the paragraph and questions again. If you still don't understand the answers and the reasons for them, check with your teacher before going on.

# PART FOUR

# *Practice Exercises*

The thirty exercises that follow will help you use your ability to understand organization and make summaries.

Each exercise is like the sample in Part Three.

Read each passage well. Answer the questions carefully and thoughtfully. Correct your answers, using the answer key at the back of the book. Mark your scores on the chart on the inside back cover before going on to the next exercise.

# · 1 ·

There are many kinds of snakes. Often their names describe them. Some snakes are named for their colors, such as green, scarlet, and coral snakes. Often snakes are named for physical features. There are short-tailed snakes and sharp-tailed snakes. There are also flat-headed snakes. Some snakes are named for the patterns of scales on their heads. They have names such as cone, hog, hook, and leaf snakes.

Snakes kept as pets are often quiet and tame. They do not tend to attack as they might if they were in the wild. People who have snakes as pets think each snake has its own personality.

1. In the first paragraph the author organizes examples of snakes and their names by using
   ☐ a. simple listing.
   ☐ b. order of importance.
   ☐ c. time order.
   ☐ d. space order.

2. This passage states that
   ☐ a. most snakes are dangerous.
   ☐ b. snakes are found all over the Americas.
   ☐ c. snakes are related to lizards.
   ☐ d. the names of snakes often describe them.

3. Which is the best summary of the *second* paragraph?
   ☐ a. Snakes kept as pets do not tend to attack as they might if they were in the wild.
   ☐ b. Pet snakes are often quiet and tame and seem to have personalities.
   ☐ c. Pet snakes need care and attention.
   ☐ d. Snakes are better off in the wild than as pets.

4. Underline examples of snakes named for patterns of scales on their heads.

# ·2·

Long ago most people did not have last names. People lived in small villages. Everyone in the village knew everyone else. One name was enough. The custom of second names began in Europe around 1200. People were beginning to travel, and towns were getting bigger. Second names became useful. They helped strangers learn more about the people they met. The second names were passed down from parent to child.

Some names told about jobs. An example is *Alice the cook*. That name became *Alice Cook*. Other names told where people lived. *Mary at the wood* became *Mary Atwood*. The most common names told about people's fathers, such as the name *Tom, John's son*. That name became *Tom Johnson*.

Second names developed in the same way in other countries. In Ireland *Anna O'Donald* means "Anna of the family of Donald." In Russia *Ivan Petrov* means "Ivan, son of Peter." And in Italy *Maria DeStefano* means "Maria, daughter of Stefano."

1. In the first paragraph the author explains why second names came to be. He or she uses
   - ☐ a. time order.
   - ☐ b. cause and effect.
   - ☐ c. space order.
   - ☐ d. comparison.

2. In the second paragraph the author shows which kind of name was most common. He or she uses
   - ☐ a. time order.
   - ☐ b. space order.
   - ☐ c. simple listing.
   - ☐ d. order of importance.

3. This passage states that
   - ☐ a. some last names told where people lived.
   - ☐ b. last names have been used longer than first names.
   - ☐ c. the Italians invented the custom of last names.
   - ☐ d. last names began in Asia.

4. Underline the sentence that explains the beginnings of a name like Lois Carpenter.

# ·3·

The word *palindrome* (PAL-uhn-drohm) comes from the Greek language. It means "running back again." A palindrome can be a word, number, or sentence. But it must read the same backward or forward.

Many words are palindromes. *Did* is one. So are *noon* and *peep.* Names can be palindromes. Think of *Eve, Bob,* and *Hannah.* The most interesting palindromes are sentences. *Madam, I'm Adam* is a well-known palindrome.

Napoleon was a French emperor. He inspired a palindrome. In 1814 he was sent to live on an island called Elba. Someone made up a palindrome about him. It is *Able was I ere I saw Elba.* (*Ere* means "before.")

1. This passage states that
   - ☐ a. names can be palindromes.
   - ☐ b. *palindrome* was a Latin word.
   - ☐ c. Napoleon wrote the first palindromes.
   - ☐ d. short palindromes are the hardest to create.

2. In the second paragraph the author argues that sentence palindromes are most interesting. The organization is
   - ☐ a. space order.
   - ☐ b. simple listing.
   - ☐ c. cause and effect.
   - ☐ d. order of importance.

3. Which is the best summary of the passage?
   - ☐ a. A palindrome is a word, number, or sentence that can be read backward or forward.
   - ☐ b. A palindrome like *Madam, I'm Adam* reads the same backward or forward.
   - ☐ c. Words and sentences can be palindromes.
   - ☐ d. Napoleon's story inspired a long palindrome.

4. Underline a sentence that tells why *palindrome* makes a good name for the words and sentences discussed in the passage.

# ·4·

Few fish match the trout for natural beauty and grace. Trout are in the salmon family. They are powerful fighters when hooked.

Trout change appearance depending on where they live. The nature of the water makes a difference. So does the type of stream or lake bed and the food the trout eat.

Freshwater trout and sea trout are different forms of the same species. A freshwater trout lives all its life in fresh water. A sea trout feeds in the sea. It enters its home stream in summer to breed in autumn. Adult sea trout are often longer than freshwater trout. But it still may be difficult to tell these two forms apart. Sea trout darken when they have been in fresh water for a few weeks. Then they look like freshwater trout.

1. In the third paragraph the author shows how the two trout differ. The organization is
   □ a. time order.
   □ c. space order.
   □ b. cause and effect.
   □ d. contrast.

2. This passage states that
   □ a. trout are in the mackerel family.
   □ b. all trout look the same.
   □ c. people should avoid eating sea trout.
   □ d. trout change their appearance.

3. Which is the best summary of the *third* paragraph?
   □ a. Freshwater trout live in fresh water. Sea trout live in the sea part of the time. After a sea trout has been in fresh water, it looks like a freshwater trout.
   □ b. Freshwater trout and sea trout are different forms of the same species. The freshwater trout lives all its life in fresh water. The sea trout feeds in the sea.
   □ c. Sea trout darken when they have been in fresh water. Then they look like freshwater trout.
   □ d. The sea trout feeds in the sea. It enters its home stream in summer to breed in autumn.

4. Underline a sentence that tells why the sea trout returns to the stream where it was hatched.

# · 5 ·

The purple finch and the pine grosbeak are wild birds. They are often mistaken for each other.

The purple finch is about six inches (fifteen centimeters) long. *Purple* is a strange word for it. It is dark pink. Its head and back are brightly colored. The bird looks like a sparrow dipped in raspberry juice. The male has brighter color than the female. Its song is a fast, lively warble. The notes sound like *tick, tick, tick.*

The male pine grosbeak is also dark pink. But it has white wing bars. Its song is different, too. It is a clear three-note warble. The notes sound like *tee, tee, tew.* Unlike the shy finch, grosbeaks are often quite tame and bold. Perhaps this is because they are larger. Grosbeaks are almost ten inches (twenty-five centimeters) long.

1. The author shows how the finch and grosbeak differ. The details are organized by
   ☐ a. simple listing.
   ☐ b. cause and effect.
   ☐ c. time order.
   ☐ d. contrast.

2. This passage states that the
   ☐ a. purple finch is actually pink.
   ☐ b. male grosbeak is smaller than the finch.
   ☐ c. purple finch is a bold bird.
   ☐ d. finch and grosbeak have the same song.

3. Which is the best summary of the passage?
   ☐ a. Grosbeaks are dark pink. They are almost ten inches (twenty-five centimeters) long.
   ☐ b. The purple finch looks like a sparrow dipped in raspberry juice. Its song is a fast, lively warble.
   ☐ c. The grosbeak is dark pink like the purple finch, but it is larger and bolder, and it has a different call.
   ☐ d. The finch and the grosbeak are wild birds.

4. Underline the sentences that describe the songs of the two birds.

# ·6·

The year was 1903. Orville Wright flew his plane at Kitty Hawk. Five people watched. No reporters gathered facts. No one snapped photos. No one seemed to care about the feat at all. One well-known magazine did mention the flight. It suggested that the flight was a fake. The public was still charmed by the automobile. It did not consider the airplane a means of travel.

Charles Lindbergh changed all that. His flight from New York to Paris thrilled people throughout the world. Newspapers used more than twenty-five thousand tons of newsprint to report it. Radio stations spread the news. Details were heard from coast to coast and around the world. The year was 1927. The aviation industry would never be the same again.

1. The author organizes details by time order and
   □ a. simple listing.
   □ b. cause and effect.
   □ c. space order.
   □ d. contrast.

2. This passage states that
   □ a. radio stations covered Wright's flight.
   □ b. Orville Wright's flight was a fake.
   □ c. five people watched Orville Wright fly.
   □ d. Lindbergh's flight went unnoticed.

3. Which is the best summary of the passage?
   □ a. In 1903 Orville Wright's airplane flight was almost ignored. In 1927 Charles Lindbergh's flight caught the attention of the whole world.
   □ b. Orville Wright flew at Kitty Hawk in 1903. A well-known magazine mentioned the flight.
   □ c. The public was charmed by the automobile. It did not consider the airplane a means of travel. Charles Lindbergh changed all that.
   □ d. Charles Lindbergh flew from New York to Paris in 1927.

4. Underline a sentence that tells why people around the world were able to hear the details of Lindbergh's flight.

# · 7 ·

Anyone who can follow directions can do a magic trick. But learning a trick is the easy part. To be a magician, you need to master a certain style.

You must be calm. Practice each trick so that you know it inside and out. Don't get nervous; don't worry. Then work slowly. Many new magicians make the mistake of working too fast. They want to prove that the hand is faster than the eye. That is not always so.

Learn to talk in a steady stream. A good magician chatters and chatters. This distracts the audience. It gets them thinking of something else. In that state, they can be fooled.

The most important thing you need is nerve, and plenty of it. Magic is mostly bluff, so you must be confident. Stand up tall, talk in a calm voice, and dazzle your audience with mystery.

1. The author organizes the passage as a whole by
   - ☐ a. simple listing.
   - ☐ b. time order.
   - ☐ c. order of importance.
   - ☐ d. space order.

2. The author organizes details in the third paragraph by
   - ☐ a. cause and effect.
   - ☐ b. comparison.
   - ☐ c. space order.
   - ☐ d. contrast.

3. Which is the best summary of the passage?
   - ☐ a. To be a good magician, be calm. Don't get nervous; don't worry.
   - ☐ b. To be a good magician, practice, stay calm, keep chattering, and most importantly, be confident.
   - ☐ c. To be a good magician, chatter and chatter. This distracts the audience.
   - ☐ d. To be a good magician, you need nerve, and plenty of it. To bluff, you must be confident.

4. Underline the sentences that tell why a good magician keeps up a stream of chatter.

# ·8·

Many home gardeners don't grow corn. They say that the small amount of corn they get isn't worth the room the plants take up in the garden. I disagree. The amount of corn can be increased with a little work and thought.

Corn needs rich soil. Hundreds of years ago, native Americans solved that problem. They put a dead fish into the ground with every kernel of corn. You probably don't have a large supply of dead fish on hand. Instead, fill each hole with compost. Then add lots of fertilizer.

Plan the shape of your corn section. Corn is pollinated by the wind. If it's planted in a long row, the wind carries the pollen away. I plant my corn in four short rows. The wind spreads pollen from one row to the next. I also plant four different kinds of corn. That brings different harvest times, instead of more corn than I can handle all at once.

1. The author organizes details mainly by
   - ☐ a. time order.
   - ☐ b. comparison.
   - ☐ c. cause and effect.
   - ☐ d. contrast.

2. This passage states that corn
   - ☐ a. isn't worth planting in home gardens.
   - ☐ b. needs rich soil.
   - ☐ c. will not grow well unless it is planted with dead fish.
   - ☐ d. should be planted in one long row.

3. Which is the best summary of the passage?
   - ☐ a. Corn will grow well if you fertilize it and plant it in short rows so that it will pollinate.
   - ☐ b. Many home gardeners don't grow corn. But the yield of corn plants can be increased.
   - ☐ c. If you don't have dead fish on hand, use compost and fertilizer.
   - ☐ d. Plant four different kinds of corn for different harvest times.

4. Underline a sentence that tells how native Americans solved the problem of fertilizing corn.

# ·9·

The people of ancient times noticed that the stars in the sky seemed to circle the Earth all at once. They seemed to be pinned, or fixed, to the turning sky. They were called the "fixed stars."

But seven objects in the sky did not move with the stars. Two of the objects were the sun and the moon. The other five were dots of light like the stars, but brighter. These seven objects changed position with respect to the stars. Night after night, they followed paths of their own. The objects were called "planets." The name came from a Greek word that means "wandering." The people named the five starlike planets after gods. Like gods, the planets seemed to do anything they wished.

1. The author organizes the passage as a whole by
   ☐ a. simple listing.
   ☐ b. order of importance.
   ☐ c. space order.
   ☐ d. contrast.

2. The author organizes details in each paragraph by
   ☐ a. time order.
   ☐ b. cause and effect.
   ☐ c. comparison and contrast.
   ☐ d. comparison.

3. The passage states that
   ☐ a. the sun is actually a planet.
   ☐ b. people of ancient times did not understand that the Earth turns on its axis.
   ☐ c. the Earth spins around the other planets.
   ☐ d. people of ancient times called some objects in the sky planets because they seemed to wander.

4. Underline a sentence that tells why the people named the planets after gods.

# · 10 ·

The tin can was invented in 1812. It was not widely used until 1847. That year a machine was built that could make tin cans cheaply. A whole new food business was born. Two of the first foods to be canned were oysters and tomatoes. Miners took canned food along to the Gold Rush. Then the Civil War broke out. The need for canned food soared. Unlike fresh foods, canned foods would not spoil. Therefore, huge crates of canned milk and beans were shipped to the troops. After the war, canned food became popular in homes.

Attempts to freeze foods began in the mid-1800s. In 1917, Clarence Birdseye developed a "quick-freeze" process. This made packaged frozen food possible. It took another war to make it common. Frozen food is lighter than canned food. Therefore, it is easier to ship. During World War II, it was flown all over the world to feed the troops. After the war, it began to appear widely in stores.

1. The author organizes details in the first paragraph by cause and effect and by
   ☐ a. simple listing.        ☐ c. order of importance.
   ☐ b. time order.            ☐ d. space order.

2. In the passage as a whole, the writer
   ☐ a. lists examples of canned foods and frozen foods.
   ☐ b. compares the histories of canned foods and frozen foods.
   ☐ c. shows why canned foods are more popular than frozen foods.
   ☐ d. states the most important reasons for canning foods.

3. To explain why frozen food became common during World War II, the author uses contrast and
   ☐ a. order of importance.
   ☐ b. cause and effect.
   ☐ c. space order.
   ☐ d. comparison.

4. Underline a sentence that tells why the tin can began to be widely used in 1847.

# · 11 ·

Scientists once thought that the Earth was hollow. As they learned more about the Earth, they changed their minds. But the idea of a hollow Earth did not disappear completely. In the early nineteenth century, a retired United States Army captain came up with his own idea. His name was John Cleves Symmes.

Symmes believed that the Earth was hollow. He also thought that there were large holes at the Earth's poles. Through these openings, the center of the hollow Earth could be reached. He said the ocean flowed in and out of these polar holes. Those imaginary holes are now called Symmes's Holes.

1. The author organizes details in the first paragraph by
   □ a. time order.
   □ b. space order.
   □ c. comparison.
   □ d. contrast.

2. In the second paragraph the author uses
   □ a. simple listing to give examples of holes in the Earth.
   □ b. order of importance to show which holes matter most.
   □ c. time order to show how holes developed.
   □ d. space order to show where the holes were supposed to be.

3. This passage states that
   □ a. the Earth is hollow.
   □ b. Symmes explored the holes in the Earth.
   □ c. Symmes was a retired United States Army captain.
   □ d. the oceans flow from holes in the Earth.

4. Underline a sentence that tells why scientists decided that the Earth was not hollow.

# · 12 ·

Thomas Jefferson had a strong interest in native Americans. He had struggled with their problems. He was interested in their languages. Through the years, he gathered fifty native American vocabularies. He planned to have them printed side by side in columns. He wished to compare them with each other and with Russian. He hoped to find a common origin. But he never completed his plan. When he left the White House, his papers were packed in a trunk. They were supposed to be shipped to his Virginia home. Some wharf hands thought the trunk held gold. They stole the trunk and opened it. Inside they found nothing but paper. They were so angry that they ripped the sheets and tossed them into the James River. A few of the papers were recovered. They were soaked and muddy and completely useless.

1. To tell what happened to Jefferson's work, the author uses
   ☐ a. order of importance.
   ☐ b. space order.
   ☐ c. time order.
   ☐ d. comparison.

2. This passage states that
   ☐ a. Jefferson found the origin of Russian.
   ☐ b. native American languages came from Russian.
   ☐ c. Jefferson hid gold under his papers.
   ☐ d. Jefferson never completed his plan.

3. Which is the best summary of the passage?
   ☐ a. Jefferson planned to compare native American languages and Russian, but his notes were stolen.
   ☐ b. Jefferson had a long-standing interest in native Americans, their problems, and their languages.
   ☐ c. Jefferson gathered native American vocabularies to compare them with each other and with Russian.
   ☐ d. Some wharf hands stole Jefferson's papers, ripped the sheets, and tossed them into the James River.

4. Underline a sentence that tells what happened after the wharf hands found paper in the trunk.

# · 13 ·

Richard Rodgers first heard theater music at the age of two. In those days, people bought sheet music from shows the way we buy tapes and records. Rodgers's mother played the tunes on the piano. She and her husband sang along. These concerts took place for many years. It wasn't long before Richard learned the words to all the songs. At four, he was picking out notes on the piano to fit the songs. At six, he taught himself to play with both hands. His interest in music delighted his parents. He began piano lessons at once. Later he saw musical shows whenever he could scrape together the price of a ticket. Soon he began writing music. His parents urged him to pursue it as a career. As an adult, he became a famous composer of show tunes. Among his scores are *South Pacific* and *The Sound of Music.*

1. The author organizes details by
   □ a. simple listing.      □ c. order of importance.
   □ b. time order.          □ d. comparison.

2. This passage states that
   □ a. the Rodgers family had a tape recorder.
   □ b. Rodgers never learned to read music.
   □ c. Rodgers heard theater music when he was two.
   □ d. Rodgers's first show tunes were failures.

3. Which is the best summary of the passage?
   □ a. Richard Rodgers was a composer of show tunes, including *South Pacific* and *The Sound of Music.*
   □ b. By age six, Richard Rodgers had taught himself to play the piano with both hands.
   □ c. When Richard Rodgers was a child, people bought sheet music as we buy tapes and records.
   □ d. Richard Rodgers's childhood interest in music helped him become the famous composer of *South Pacific* and other shows.

4. Underline a sentence that tells what Rodgers did after he began taking piano lessons.

# · 14 ·

The term *O.K.* is one of the best-known American expressions. Many people believe that *O.K.* comes from a nickname for Martin Van Buren. Van Buren was elected president of the United States in 1836. When he ran for reelection in 1840, his supporters wanted to give him a nickname. A nickname would help voters remember him. Some people began to call Van Buren "Old Kinderhook" because he was born in Kinderhook, New York. Then several New Yorkers formed a political group called the Democratic O.K. Club. The *O.K.* stood for "Old Kinderhook." Even though Van Buren lost the election, people kept using the phrase *O.K.* Today it means "all right or correct."

1. The author organizes details in the passage by
   □ a. simple listing.
   □ b. time order.
   □ c. order of importance.
   □ d. space order.

2. What happened after Van Buren lost the election?
   □ a. People stopped using *O.K.*
   □ b. *O.K.* became a popular expression.
   □ c. He ran for president again.
   □ d. The Democratic O.K. Club voted against him.

3. This passage states that *O.K.* came from
   □ a. the Republican O.K. Club.
   □ b. a word that means "all right or correct."
   □ c. the nickname "Old Kinderhook."
   □ d. Van Buren's middle name.

4. Underline a sentence that tells what *O.K.* means today.

Though I failed to mention it in my log, I had terrible pains in my back that evening. Needling aches had plagued me for days. That night, they reached their peak. I was sore from the dampness and the lurching of the raft. My hands were raw from handling the ropes in wet, windy weather. Worse, my nose was severely sunburned. The flaky skin peeled around the nostrils. A second layer of skin was exposed. It was too tender for the blistering sun and salty breezes. None of these ailments kept me from my regular duties. But I did neglect to make my entries in my daily log for at least a week.

1. The author organizes the list of aches and pains by
   ☐ a. simple listing.
   ☐ b. time order.
   ☐ c. order of importance.
   ☐ d. comparison.

2. This passage states that
   ☐ a. the writer's boat had sunk.
   ☐ b. the writer was able to ignore his or her pain.
   ☐ c. sun and salt air hurt the writer's nose.
   ☐ d. the writer feared that the raft would sink.

3. Which is the best summary of the passage?
   ☐ a. Terrible backaches had bothered the author for days. On the night they reached their peak the writer failed to mention it in the log.
   ☐ b. After days on a raft, terrible pain, particularly from a sunburned nose, made the author neglect the log. But he or she managed to keep working.
   ☐ c. After days on a raft, the author was sore from dampness, and his or her hands were raw from handling ropes in wet, windy weather.
   ☐ d. The author's ailments did not keep him or her from regular duties. But he or she did neglect to make entries in the daily log for at least a week.

4. Underline a sentence that tells why the exposed second layer of skin hurt so much.

# · 16 ·

One day, Bob Hope was playing golf with movie producer Sam Goldwyn. On one hole, Goldwyn missed an easy putt. He became so angry that he threw his putter away in disgust. Then he turned and huffed off to the next tee. Hope picked up the putter and stuck it into his own golf bag.

On the next hole, Hope used the putter Goldwyn had thrown away. A fine golfer, Hope sank a long, difficult putt.

"That was really good," Goldwyn said. "Let me see that putter."

Goldwyn examined the club and took a few practice swings with it. Then he said to Hope, "I like this putter very much. Will you sell it to me?"

"Sure," said Hope, "but it'll cost you fifty dollars."

Goldwyn bought the putter from Hope and used it for years. He felt he'd found a real bargain.

1. The author organizes details mainly by
   ☐ a. simple listing.        ☐ c. order of importance.
   ☐ b. time order.            ☐ d. space order.

2. This passage states that Goldwyn
   ☐ a. was the better golfer.  ☐ c. bought his own putter.
   ☐ b. cheated Hope.           ☐ d. refused to play again.

3. Which is the best summary of the passage?
   ☐ a. Bob Hope and Sam Goldwyn sometimes played golf together, but Goldwyn had a short temper.
   ☐ b. When Sam Goldwyn missed an easy putt, he flew into a rage and threw his putter away. Bob Hope picked the putter up and used it as his own.
   ☐ c. Bob Hope and Sam Goldwyn had a funny game of golf that ended when Hope sold his putter.
   ☐ d. After missing a shot, Sam Goldwyn threw his putter away. Secretly, Bob Hope picked it up. He did so well with it that Goldwyn bought it from him.

4. Underline the sentence that tells what Goldwyn said right after Hope sank his putt.

In 1838 whaling was an important industry on Nantucket Island. That year a fire broke out on Main Street. A few buildings were destroyed. Eight years later, another fire destroyed the center of town. More than three hundred buildings were burned. Many businesses went up in flames.

Meanwhile, Nantucket sailors had learned about the California Gold Rush. Because the fires had destroyed so much, Nantucket was a hard place to live. Sailors wanted to look for gold. Many of them left Nantucket for the West Coast. Shipowners on the island could not find good crews. Nantucket was having terrible money troubles.

1. The author tells the story of the fires in the first paragraph. The organization is
   ☐ a. time order.
   ☐ b. cause and effect.
   ☐ c. space order.
   ☐ d. comparison.

2. The author explains why the Gold Rush hurt Nantucket in the second paragraph. The organization is
   ☐ a. simple listing.
   ☐ b. cause and effect.
   ☐ c. order of importance.
   ☐ d. contrast.

3. Which is the best summary of the passage?
   ☐ a. Fire and the California Gold Rush nearly ruined Nantucket.
   ☐ b. Eight years later, a fire destroyed the center of town.
   ☐ c. No one rebuilt Nantucket after fires nearly destroyed it.
   ☐ d. Sailors learned about the California Gold Rush.

4. Underline a sentence that tells about the shipowners.

Phineas T. Barnum gave the public great thrills. He also knew how to fool them. He is famous for saying, "There's a sucker born every minute." Barnum showed all kinds of freaks and "monsters." He attracted crowds with false ads.

He claimed to have a mermaid. It was really the upper half of a monkey's body sewed to the lower half of a fish. He promised dancing turkeys. The turkeys danced because the floor of their cage was hot. He claimed to have a "cherry-colored" cat. It was a black cat. Barnum got around that fraud by reminding people that there are black cherries. Barnum's greatest fraud was the simplest. It was a sign that pointed to a door. The sign said, "To the Egress." People thought that the Egress was another strange monster. Eagerly they poured through the door. They were disappointed to find themselves back on the street. *Egress* is another word for *exit.*

1. The author gives examples of Barnum's tricks in the second paragraph. The examples are organized by
   ☐ a. time order.　　　　☐ c. cause and effect.
   ☐ b. simple listing.　　☐ d. order of importance.

2. This passage states that
   ☐ a. furious customers demanded their money back.
   ☐ b. Barnum became wealthy by fooling the public.
   ☐ c. most people knew they were being fooled.
   ☐ d. Barnum used false advertising.

3. Which is the best summary of the passage?
   ☐ a. Among the many tricks that P. T. Barnum pulled on the public, his "Egress" fraud was the best.
   ☐ b. Phineas T. Barnum gave the public great thrills, but he also knew how to fool them.
   ☐ c. Barnum claimed to have a mermaid, but it was only a monkey's body sewed to a fish's tail.
   ☐ d. Barnum got around his "cherry-colored" cat fraud by reminding people that there are black cherries.

4. Underline a sentence that uses cause and effect to explain how Barnum made turkeys dance.

# · 19 ·

Before they had horses, native Americans had to travel on foot whenever they moved their camps. Some tribes used big shaggy dogs as pack animals. On long trips, the dogs would grow tired. They would droop and lag and hang their tongues. Someone would cry, "Buffalo ahead! Fresh meat!" The dogs would bound forward as if they had just set out.

The Spaniards brought the first horses to North America in the sixteenth century. Within a century, runaway horses had drifted northward. Wild herds roamed the plains. Native Americans learned to capture and tame those wild horses. In time, native Americans became some of the world's finest riders.

The horses changed the lives of many tribes. Now they could travel long distances to hunt the choicest buffalo. With pack horses, they could carry bigger tepees and more possessions.

1. The passage as a whole tells the story of native Americans and horses. Overall, the author organizes details by
   ☐ a. simple listing.
   ☐ b. time order.
   ☐ c. order of importance.
   ☐ d. contrast.

2. The first paragraph explains how native Americans kept their dogs moving. The author uses
   ☐ a. order of importance.
   ☐ b. cause and effect.
   ☐ c. space order.
   ☐ d. comparison.

3. The third paragraph explains how horses changed native Americans' lives. The author uses
   ☐ a. cause and effect.
   ☐ b. contrast.
   ☐ c. simple listing.
   ☐ d. time order.

4. Underline the sentence that tells when horses arrived in North America.

# · 20 ·

Angler fish use "fishing rods and lures" to catch their food. Their rods are thin sticks on their heads. The rods float ahead of the angler. Bulbs at the tips of the rods act as lures.

Anglers that live in shallow water wiggle their lures to attract prey. Other anglers live in the dark waters of deep seas. Their lures glow. Prey is attracted to the light.

The largest of the anglers is the goosefish. It is a deep-sea fish with a glowing lure. Its mouth is huge. The goosefish can swallow a fish almost as large as itself. Its sharp teeth curve back into its mouth. The prey can't escape once the goosefish has a grip on it.

1. The second paragraph shows how two kinds of anglers differ. The author uses
   ☐ a. time order.
   ☐ b. simple listing.
   ☐ c. contrast.
   ☐ d. order of importance.

2. This passage states that
   ☐ a. deep-sea anglers are the largest fish in the sea.
   ☐ b. deep-sea anglers have lures that glow.
   ☐ c. the goosefish lives in shallow waters.
   ☐ d. angler fish are an important human food.

3. Which is the best summary of the *third* paragraph?
   ☐ a. Angler fish have thin sticks called rods extending from their heads that float ahead of the angler and are used to lure prey.
   ☐ b. The goosefish is a large, deep-sea angler fish with a glowing lure, a huge mouth, and sharp, curved teeth that trap its prey.
   ☐ c. The largest of the anglers is the goosefish, a deep-sea fish with a glowing lure and a huge mouth.
   ☐ d. Thanks to its huge mouth, the goosefish can swallow a fish almost as large as itself.

4. Circle the paragraph that uses space order to describe the angler's rod and lure.

# · *21* ·

Sam Bellamy was a famous pirate. Before he became a pirate, he'd had other plans. As a young man in England, he wished to hunt treasure, not steal it. Bellamy heard of a Spanish ship that had sunk in the West Indies. It was loaded with silver coins. In 1715, he sailed west in a tiny sloop to find that treasure. He stopped at Eastham on Cape Cod to rest and obtain supplies.

For many weeks he stayed at Higgins Tavern. One spring night, under an apple tree, he met Maria Hallet. They fell in love. Bellamy vowed he'd come back and marry her when he found his treasure. Then he sailed away.

In the West Indies, Bellamy found the wreck he was looking for, but he found no treasure. He'd spent all his money in the search. He had nothing to show for it. Frustrated and impatient, he became a pirate.

1. The passage as a whole tells the story of Sam Bellamy. The author organizes details mainly by
   ☐ a. simple listing.
   ☐ b. order of importance.
   ☐ c. time order.
   ☐ d. space order.

2. The first paragraph explains why Bellamy sailed for the West Indies. The author organizes these details by
   ☐ a. time order.
   ☐ b. space order.
   ☐ c. cause and effect.
   ☐ d. comparison and contrast.

3. The third paragraph explains what made Bellamy become a pirate. The author organizes these details by
   ☐ a. cause and effect.
   ☐ b. comparison and contrast.
   ☐ c. comparison.
   ☐ d. contrast.

4. Underline a sentence that tells what happened after Bellamy vowed to return and marry Maria Hallet.

# · 22 ·

Many years ago, textile mills were built along the rivers of New England. The mills often had four to six floors. Each mill was carefully planned.

The basement housed the waterwheel. The flowing river turned the wheel to make power. The wheel was below ground for two reasons. Deep water meant greater water power. Warmth from the ground also kept water from freezing.

Raw cotton or wool came to the mill by horse and wagon. On the first floor, workers carded the wool. At first they brushed and combed the tangled fibers by hand. Later carding was done with huge machines. The material then went to the second floor. There it was spun into thread. Huge spools of thread were sent by elevator to the third floor. There weavers turned it into cloth. Finally, the cloth was sent to the fourth floor. There it was washed, pressed, and cut.

1. The author has several purposes. One is to explain why the waterwheel was in the basement. To explain that fact in the second paragraph, the author uses
   ☐ a. time order.          ☐ c. cause and effect.
   ☐ b. space order.         ☐ d. comparison and contrast.

2. Another purpose is to show the steps used to make cloth. To explain those steps in the third paragraph, the author uses
   ☐ a. simple listing.       ☐ c. order of importance.
   ☐ b. time order.           ☐ d. space order.

3. Another purpose is to show that the layout of the mill was carefully planned. Therefore, in the third paragraph the author also uses
   ☐ a. order of importance.  ☐ c. time order.
   ☐ b. space order.          ☐ d. cause and effect.

4. Underline a sentence that tells what happened on the second floor of the mill.

# · 23 ·

The whistle sign is a common feature of the railroad landscape. It is placed before highway crossings, bridges, and tunnels. It is placed wherever the tracks might be blocked by people, cars, or animals. The sign usually has a big **W** in the center, which stands for "whistle." The whistle sign tells the engineer to sound two long blasts, one short and another long.

Actually, real whistles went out with the steam engine a few decades ago. They were replaced by air horns. Air horns are just as loud as whistles. On some engines the horns even play an attractive chord. However, the steam whistle had a special, spooky, animal-like shriek. Once heard, it was not soon forgotten.

1.  In the first paragraph, the author describes the sign and its location. The organization is
    ☐ a. time order.
    ☐ b. space order.
    ☐ c. cause and effect.
    ☐ d. order of importance.

2.  In the second paragraph, the author discusses whistles and air horns. The organization is
    ☐ a. simple listing.
    ☐ b. time order.
    ☐ c. cause and effect.
    ☐ d. comparison and contrast.

3.  This passage states that
    ☐ a. whistle signs are no longer seen today.
    ☐ b. the most common whistle message is one long blast.
    ☐ c. air horns can play an attractive chord.
    ☐ d. whistles replaced the older air horns.

4.  Underline a sentence that tells where you can see whistle signs.

# · 24 ·

In 1835 the *New York Sun* surprised the world with a major story. It reported that an English astronomer, Sir John Herschel, had discovered life on the moon. Then it described the creatures in detail. They had furry bodies and batlike wings.

Many newspapers picked up the story. For weeks everyone buzzed with the startling news. Then a group of scientists from Yale went to New York. They asked the *Sun* to show them Herschel's report. Under pressure, the *Sun* admitted the truth. Sir John Herschel was out of the country and didn't know about the *Sun's* articles. The whole scoop was false.

By that time, circulation of the *Sun* had soared. Overnight it had become the best-selling paper in the United States.

1. The passage tells the story of a trick. The author organizes details by
   ☐ a. time order.
   ☐ b. space order.
   ☐ c. cause and effect.
   ☐ d. contrast.

2. This passage states that
   ☐ a. Herschel had made an honest mistake.
   ☐ b. Herschel was a scientist at Yale.
   ☐ c. the *Sun* had been fooled by Herschel.
   ☐ d. Sir John Herschel didn't know about the *Sun's* articles.

3. Which is the best summary of the passage?
   ☐ a. In 1835 the *New York Sun* surprised the world with a major story about life on the moon.
   ☐ b. In 1835 a trick about life on the moon made the *New York Sun* the best-selling paper in the United States.
   ☐ c. In 1835 the English astronomer Sir John Herschel discovered furry creatures on the moon.
   ☐ d. In 1835 a group of scientists from Yale went to New York to review Sir John Herschel's report.

4. Underline a sentence that tells what happened as a result of the *Sun's* story.

Most ants live in large colonies. Most of these colonies are under ground. The ants build large "cities" in the earth. Big cones of dirt and pine needles are piled above their nests. The ants spend the day foraging for food above ground.

Some ants build their homes in trees or wood. Still others build their nests of leaves. The ants sew the leaves together with silk made by grubs. Then there are the army ants of the tropics. They don't make nests at all. They march at night in huge columns. They camp during the day in some sheltered spot. There the whole group of ants clings together. They make a nest of their bodies. The queens and brood stay in the center.

1. The author shows different ways that ants live. Details are organized by
   ☐ a. time order.
   ☐ b. comparison and contrast.
   ☐ c. simple listing.
   ☐ d. order of importance.

2. This passage states that
   ☐ a. some ants build nests of leaves.
   ☐ b. most ants live in small family groups.
   ☐ c. all ants make their homes in wood.
   ☐ d. army ants have powerful stingers.

3. Which is the best summary of the passage?
   ☐ a. Most ants live in large colonies under ground, which are like large "cities" in the earth.
   ☐ b. Some ants live under ground, but others build their homes in trees or leaves.
   ☐ c. The army ants of the tropics march at night and camp during the day.
   ☐ d. Most ants live in large colonies under ground, in trees, in nests of leaves, or on the move in armies.

4. Underline a sentence that tells where the army ants make their camps.

# · 26 ·

In the summer of 1874, grasshoppers invaded Kansas. Quite suddenly, the air was filled with them. People likened the attack to a snowstorm. Tree limbs snapped under the weight of the insects. Every bush was covered with them and then instantly devoured. Quickly and cleanly, they ate everything in their path. Whole fields of wheat and corn disappeared. Even root plants such as potatoes and carrots were eaten. The farmers tried to fight back. They covered the remaining crops with quilts and sheets. The grasshoppers ate right through them. Once every green plant was gone, the grass-hoppers moved to the farm buildings. They ate everything made of wood. Fences disappeared, and siding was stripped off barns and homes. Indoors, they ate their way through kitchens. Then they destroyed furniture, clothing, and curtains.

1. The author tells the story of the attack of the grasshoppers. Details are organized by
   ☐ a. order of importance.  ☐ c. time order.
   ☐ b. space order.  ☐ d. contrast.

2. This passage states that the grasshoppers
   ☐ a. ate everything in their path.
   ☐ b. were driven away by the farmers.
   ☐ c. left after eating the wheat and corn.
   ☐ d. avoided places where people lived.

3. Which is the best summary of the passage?
   ☐ a. So many grasshoppers invaded Kansas that the attack looked like a snowstorm.
   ☐ b. In Kansas, invading grasshoppers once ate crops, buildings, fences, and household goods.
   ☐ c. When grasshoppers invaded, they ate whole fields of wheat, corn, potatoes, and carrots.
   ☐ d. Invading grasshoppers ate everything made of wood, including fences, siding, and furniture.

4. Underline a sentence that tells what the grasshoppers did after they ate all the plants.

# · 27 ·

The word *panic* means "sudden and unreasonable fear." *Panic* comes from *Pan,* the name of the Greek god of woods and pastures.

According to myths, Pan startled people. His body was covered with hair. He had the feet, legs, ears, and horns of a goat! Pan was a mischievous creature. People walking in the wood were startled by the flutelike music of Pan's famous pipes. Pan also loved to appear and disappear suddenly. Myths say that his appearances made people stampede like cattle. He was also fond of making weird and scary noises in the night.

1. The author explains how *panic* got its meaning. The organization of the passage is mainly
   □ a. order of importance.
   □ b. time order.
   □ c. space order.
   □ d. cause and effect.

2. This passage states that
   □ a. *panic* means "to startle people."
   □ b. Pan was part human and part god.
   □ c. myths about Pan say that he startled people.
   □ d. Pan comforted people who were lost in the woods.

3. Which is the best summary of the passage?
   □ a. The word *panic* comes from the name of a Greek god and means "sudden fear."
   □ b. According to myths, Pan startled people because he had the feet, legs, ears, and horns of a goat.
   □ c. Pan's sudden appearances and the weird noises he made in the night add to the meaning of a modern word.
   □ d. The startling looks and actions of the Greek god Pan gave us *panic,* our word for "sudden fear."

4. Underline a sentence that tells what caused people to stampede like cattle.

# · 28 ·

There are three types of avalanches. The least dangerous type is a mass of heavy, wet snow. It can move down a mountain at speeds of up to twenty miles per hour (32 kph).

Avalanches of dry, powdery snow are more dangerous. They move at speeds of up to two hundred miles per hour (320 kph). Shock waves go before them. These shock waves are very strong. They can knock down buildings before the mass of snow arrives. The powdery snow of this kind of avalanche can be compared to a dust storm. The snow is so fine that it can get into a person's lungs. It will suffocate anyone in the path of the avalanche.

The most dangerous avalanches are slab avalanches. The entire snow cover of a mountain breaks up. It then moves as a solid river of ice and snow. It buries everything in its path.

1. The author has several purposes. One is to rank avalanches according to their danger. To do this, the author uses
   □ a. order of importance.
   □ b. time order.
   □ c. space order.
   □ d. cause and effect.

2. Another purpose is to show how kinds of avalanches are alike and different. To do this, the author uses
   □ a. simple listing.
   □ b. order of importance.
   □ c. cause and effect.
   □ d. comparison and contrast.

3. This passage states that
   □ a. heavy, wet avalanches are most dangerous.
   □ b. dry, powdery avalanches are most dangerous.
   □ c. slab avalanches are most dangerous.
   □ d. all avalanches are equally dangerous.

4. Underline two sentences that explain the danger from shock waves.

# · 29 ·

Every age has its legendary heroes. Some are real. Others are made up. Each of them stands for the dreams and ambitions of a culture. For example, the ancient Jews had Samson. He tore a lion apart with his bare hands. He killed a thousand enemies with the jawbone of a donkey. The English had King Arthur and Robin Hood. The French had Joan of Arc. She led a small army to victory in a battle against the English. The Americans had Davy Crockett and Paul Bunyan. The Greeks had Hercules. Hercules was probably the greatest hero of all time. He was so strong that the gods asked him to help them in their battle against the Titans. The gods treated him as their equal, though he belonged to the world of humans.

1. The author organizes details by comparison, contrast, and
   - ☐ a. simple listing.
   - ☐ b. time order.
   - ☐ c. order of importance.
   - ☐ d. space order.

2. This passage states that an English hero was
   - ☐ a. Samson.
   - ☐ b. Joan of Arc.
   - ☐ c. Robin Hood.
   - ☐ d. Hercules.

3. Which is the best summary of the passage?
   - ☐ a. Every age has its legendary heroes. Some are real. Others are made up. Each of them stands for the dreams and ambitions of a culture.
   - ☐ b. The legendary hero of the ancient Jews was Samson. The English had King Arthur and Robin Hood. The French had Joan of Arc. The Americans had Davy Crockett and Paul Bunyan. The Greeks had Hercules.
   - ☐ c. Every age has legendary heroes. Each represents a culture. Samson and Joan of Arc were examples. Hercules was probably the greatest of all.
   - ☐ d. Hercules was so strong that the gods asked him to help them in their battle against the Titans.

4. Underline a sentence that shows what the gods thought of Hercules.

# · 30 ·

The agouti (uh-GOOT-ee) is a rodent that lives in Central and South America. It looks like a long-legged guinea pig.

The agouti's head resembles a rat's. It has a pointed snout and small, rounded ears. Its body is covered with coarse brown hair. One species has white stripes running down its back. The hair on an agouti's hindquarters is longer than the hair on its back. That long hair is usually bright orange. But it may be white or black. The agouti's body ends in a short, hairless tail. It has five toes on each front foot and three on each rear foot. Each toe has a claw.

1. The author organizes details by
   ☐ a. simple listing.
   ☐ b. order of importance.
   ☐ c. time order.
   ☐ d. space order.

2. This passage states that the
   ☐ a. agouti's hair stands up when the animal is frightened.
   ☐ b. agouti has large ears.
   ☐ c. agouti's dark colors make it hard to see.
   ☐ d. agouti's toes have claws.

3. One agouti has white stripes
   ☐ a. across its head.
   ☐ b. down its back.
   ☐ c. along its legs.
   ☐ d. across its chest.

4. Underline a sentence that compares the hair on two parts of the agouti.

# PART FIVE

# *Writing Activities*

The writing activities that follow will help you understand the organization of paragraphs. The activities will also help you organize the paragraphs *you* write.

Follow the directions. Then answer each question carefully. Sometimes your teacher may ask you to work alone. Sometimes he or she may ask you to work with other students.

You will need to write your answers on separate paper. Your teacher may ask you to write those answers in a notebook or journal. Then all your writing activities will be in the same place.

The activities in each book get harder as you go along. Look back at the activity you have already finished before you begin a new one. If you have questions about paragraph organization, reread the lesson in Parts One and Two (pages 5–14).

## ▪ *Writing Activity 1* ▪

Read the following passage from "Bad Blood" by Debra Doyle and J. D. Macdonald.

Night falls earlier than you'd expect, up in the mountains. By the time we'd finished eating dinner and cleaned up afterward, the sun had gone down and a few stars had started to come out. We built our little cookfire into a big yellow blaze, and settled down around the firepit to tell scary stories.

Mr. Castillo started things off with the story about the golden arm. That one's so old I think I first heard it back in third grade, but he did a good job all the same. When he shouted "YOU HAVE IT!" everybody jumped about a foot into the air and then pretended they hadn't.

After that Mrs. Castillo yawned and said it was about time the old folks went to bed.

A. Answer each of the following questions. Write your answers on a separate piece of paper or in your writing notebook. Your teacher may ask you to talk about your answers with the class.

1. What words in the passage tell you about the time of day? Does the story take place in the morning? Late at night? Early in the evening? How can you tell?

2. What happens after the campers finish eating dinner? What do they do next?

3. What does Mrs. Castillo do after her husband finishes telling the story?

4. The details in the passage are organized in time order. How can you tell?

B. Imagine that you are listening to Mr. Castillo's scary story about the golden arm. What are you doing as he talks? How do you feel when he first begins to tell the story? How do your feelings change as he gets closer to the end of the story?

List your ideas on a separate piece of paper or in your writing notebook.

Now rewrite your list in time order. What happens first, second, third, and fourth?

Your teacher may ask you to share your list with the class.

# ▪ *Writing Activity 2* ▪

Read the following passage about Harriet Tubman.

Harriet Tubman (1820?–1913) was born a slave in Maryland. In 1849 she escaped to Philadelphia, but she promised to return and help other slaves. During the 1850s, she returned to the South nineteen times and helped nearly 300 slaves escape. Tubman was never caught, and she never lost anyone she tried to help. During the Civil War, she worked for the Union Army as a scout, a spy, and a nurse. At the same time she helped more than 750 slaves escape from North Carolina. Today we remember Harriet Tubman's bravery. We also remember her love of freedom. But most important, we remember that she shared her love of freedom with hundreds of people who needed her help.

A. Answer each of the following questions. Write your answers on a separate piece of paper or in your writing notebook. Your teacher may ask you to talk about your answers with the class.

   1. What facts do you learn about Harriet Tubman?

   2. Which fact does the writer think is most important? What words in the sentence give you a clue?

   3. Where does the most important detail appear in the paragraph?

   4. The author also organizes the paragraph by time order. How can you tell? What facts show the passage of time?

B. Imagine that you are sitting next to a friend at the dinner table. Suddenly he or she chokes on a piece of food.
   List three things you do to help your friend. Write your list on a separate piece of paper or in your writing notebook.
   Now rewrite your list. Put the most important item last. Use your list to help you write a paragraph about saving your friend's life. Your paragraph should be at least three sentences long.
   The sentences should be arranged in order of importance. You might want to begin one sentence with the words "Most important."

## ▪ *Writing Activity 3* ▪

Read the following passage about Clarence Adams.

Clarence Adams worked as a librarian in the small Vermont town of Chester. He was a local selectman [council member] and a member of the state senate. A wealthy man, he owned a small farm a few miles from town. Everyone in Chester thought Clarence was a quiet, studious, dependable citizen.

For several years a burglar had been robbing local homes and businesses. The thief stole odd things—a bag of grain, a suit of clothes, some cheap jewelry. He rarely stole anything valuable, but he scared people. The police assumed that the burglar was someone from outside the town. They arrested several tramps and even sent some of them to jail. But the burglaries didn't stop.

Finally, the owner of the feed store decided to catch the burglar. He set up a spring-loaded gun aimed at the door of his store. The next day he discovered that the gun had gone off. The thief had been shot. Sure enough, a local man was discovered in bed with a bullet wound in his leg. The man was Clarence Adams!

A. Answer each of the following questions. Write your answers on a separate piece of paper or in your writing notebook. Your teacher may ask you to talk about your answers with the class.

   1. A tramp is a homeless person who wanders from place to place. Tramps are usually poor, and they often beg for money. Contrast Clarence Adams with a tramp. How is he different from a tramp?

   2. Most burglars steal valuable items, such as antiques or money. Contrast the burglar in this passage with the burglars you usually hear about. How is this burglar different?

B. Complete each of the following sentences. Think about cause and effect as you work. How does one event affect another?

1. Because the owner of the feed store wanted to catch the

   burglar, he _____ .

2. Clarence Adams had been shot in the leg. Therefore, the

   people of Chester knew _____ .

C. Imagine that you are a police officer. You are trying to catch a burglar who has been breaking into houses. You don't want to shoot the thief. You just want to catch him or her.

   Open your writing notebook. Write down this phrase: "If I were trying to catch a thief. . . ." Think of that phrase as a *cause*. Now list four *effects* that show how you would catch the thief.

   Remember, a *cause* is an event that makes another event occur. An *effect* is the result.

## ▪ *Writing Activity 4* ▪

Read the following passage from "Young Reverend Zelma Lee Moses" by Joyce Carol Thomas.

The owl peered through the budding branches until he focused on the kitchen, in which a mother, brown and fluffy as buttermilk biscuits, stood by the muslin-draped window, opening glass jars of yams, okra, tomatoes, spinach, and cabbage and stirred the muted [toned down] colors in a big, black cast-iron pot. . . .

When it was time, she ladled [dipped] the stew onto warmed platters, sliced warm-smelling red-pepper corn bread into generous wedges, and poured golden tea into three fat clay mugs.

A. Answer each of the following questions. Write your answers on a separate piece of paper or in your writing notebook. Your teacher may ask you to talk about your answers with the class.

1. The story is told by an owl looking in the window. Does the owl see a peaceful scene or a scary scene? How can you tell?

2. What room is the mother in? Where is she standing in the room?

3. What words make the mother sound nice? What words make the food sound good?

4. The author uses space order to describe the room and the food. How does space order help you understand the passage?

5. The author also uses time order. How can you tell?

B. Think of your kitchen at suppertime. What does it look like? What does it smell like? What objects, furniture, and appliances do you see?

Make a list of your ideas. Write the list on a separate piece of paper or in your writing notebook. Then use your list to help you write a paragraph about your kitchen.

The paragraph should be at least four sentences long. Remember to organize it in space order. Show how your kitchen looks, sounds, and smells.

# ANSWER KEY

## Practice Exercise 1
1. a       2. d       3. b
4. cone, hog, hook, and leaf snakes

## Practice Exercise 2
1. b       2. d       3. a
4. Some names told about jobs.

## Practice Exercise 3
1. a       2. d       3. b
4. It means "running back again."

## Practice Exercise 4
1. d       2. d       3. a
4. It enters its home stream in summer to breed in autumn.

## Practice Exercise 5
1. d       2. a       3. c
4. Its song is a fast, lively warble. The notes sound like *tick, tick, tick*. It is a clear three-note warble. The notes sound like *tee, tee, tew*.

## Practice Exercise 6

1. d        2. c        3. a
4. Newspapers used more than twenty-five thousand tons of newsprint to report it; *or,* Radio stations spread the news.

## Practice Exercise 7

1. c        2. a        3. b
4. This distracts the audience. It gets them thinking of something else. In that state, they can be fooled.

## Practice Exercise 8

1. c        2. b        3. a
4. They put a dead fish into the ground with every kernel of corn.

## Practice Exercise 9

1. d        2. b        3. d
4. Like gods, the planets seemed to do anything they wished.

## Practice Exercise 10

1. b        2. b        3. b
4. That year a machine was built that could make tin cans cheaply.

## Practice Exercise 11

1. a        2. d        3. c
4. As they learned more about the Earth, they changed their minds.

## Practice Exercise 12

1. c        2. d        3. a
4. They were so angry that they ripped the sheets and tossed them into the James River.

## Practice Exercise 13

1. b 　　　　2. c 　　　　3. d
4. Later he saw musical shows whenever he could scrape together the price of a ticket.

## Practice Exercise 14

1. b 　　　　2. b 　　　　3. c
4. Today it means "all right or correct."

## Practice Exercise 15

1. c 　　　　2. c 　　　　3. b
4. It was too tender for the blistering sun and salty breezes.

## Practice Exercise 16

1. b 　　　　2. c 　　　　3. d
4. "That was really good," Goldwyn said.

## Practice Exercise 17

1. a 　　　　2. b 　　　　3. a
4. Shipowners on the island could not find good crews.

## Practice Exercise 18

1. d 　　　　2. d 　　　　3. b
4. The turkeys danced because the floor of their cage was hot.

## Practice Exercise 19

1. b 　　　　2. b 　　　　3. a
4. The Spaniards brought the first horses to North America in the sixteenth century.

## Practice Exercise 20
1. c         2. b         3. b
4. Circle the first paragraph.

## Practice Exercise 21
1. c         2. c         3. a
4. Then he sailed away.

## Practice Exercise 22
1. c         2. b         3. b
4. There it was spun into thread.

## Practice Exercise 23
1. b         2. d         3. c
4. It is placed before highway crossings, bridges, and tunnels; *or,*
   It is placed wherever the tracks might be blocked by people,
   cars, or animals.

## Practice Exercise 24
1. a         2. d         3. b
4. By that time, circulation of the *Sun* had soared; *or,* Overnight
   it had become the best-selling paper in the United States.

## Practice Exercise 25
1. b         2. a         3. d
4. They camp during the day in some sheltered spot.

## Practice Exercise 26
1. c         2. a         3. b
4. Once every green plant was gone, the grasshoppers moved to
   the farm buildings.

## Practice Exercise 27

1. d            2. c            3. d

4. Myths say that his appearances made people stampede like cattle.

## Practice Exercise 28

1. a            2. d            3. c

4. These shock waves are very strong. They can knock down buildings before the mass of snow arrives.

## Practice Exercise 29

1. c            2. c            3. c

4. The gods treated him as their equal, though he belonged to the world of humans.

## Practice Exercise 30

1. d            2. d            3. b

4. The hair on an agouti's hindquarters is longer than the hair on its back.